REVIEW COPY
COURTESY OF
CAPSTONE PRESS

EDGE
BOOKS

THE WORLD'S TOP TENS

THE WORLD'S

MOST AMAZING

SURVIVAL STORIES

by Tim O'Shei

Consultant:

Al Siebert, PhD

Author of *The Survivor Personality*

Capstone
press

Mankato, Minnesota

Edge Books are published by Capstone Press,
151 Good Counsel Drive, P.O. Box 669, Mankato, Minnesota 56002.
www.capstonepress.com

Library of Congress Cataloging-in-Publication Data
O'Shei, Tim.
    The world's most amazing survival stories / by Tim O'Shei.
    p. cm.—(Edge Books. The world's top tens)
    Summary: "Describes 10 of the world's most amazing survival stories in a countdown
format"—Provided by publisher.
    Includes bibliographical references and index.
    ISBN-13: 978-0-7368-6437-4 (hardcover)
    ISBN-10: 0-7368-6437-7 (hardcover)
    1. Heroes—Biography—Juvenile literature. 2. Adventure and
adventurers—Biography—Juvenile literature. 3. Survival—Juvenile literature.
4. Courage—Juvenile literature. I. Title. II. Series.
CT107.O84 2007
920.02—dc22   2006003286

Editorial Credits
Angie Kaelberer, editor; Kate Opseth, set designer; PhaseOne, book designer;
    Wanda Winch, photo researcher; Scott Thoms, photo editor

Photo Credits
© Benjamin Mendlowitz, 19, 27 (middle left)
Corbis/Group of Survivors, 22, 27 (bottom left); Ralph White, 4
Getty Images Inc./AFP/Patrick Hertzog, 10, 26 (bottom left); Robyn Beck, 16,
    27 (top right); Steve Helber, 12, 26 (bottom right)
Globe Photos/Paul Schmulbach, 8, 26 (top right)
Noah Hamilton Photography, cover, 14, 27 (top left)
Photo courtesy of Aron Ralston, 24, 27 (bottom right)
Photo courtesy of Colby Coombs, 21, 27 (middle right)
Photo courtesy of the Gareth Wood Collection, 6, 7, 26 (top left)
Rex Rystedt Photography, SeattlePhoto, 20
SuperStock/age fotostock, 29

Consultant Al Siebert, PhD, is director of The Resiliency Center and author of
The Survivor Personality and *The Resiliency Advantage*. Web sites: http://www.
resiliencycenter.com and http://www.survivorguidelines.org

1 2 3 4 5 6 11 10 09 08 07 06

TABLE OF CONTENTS

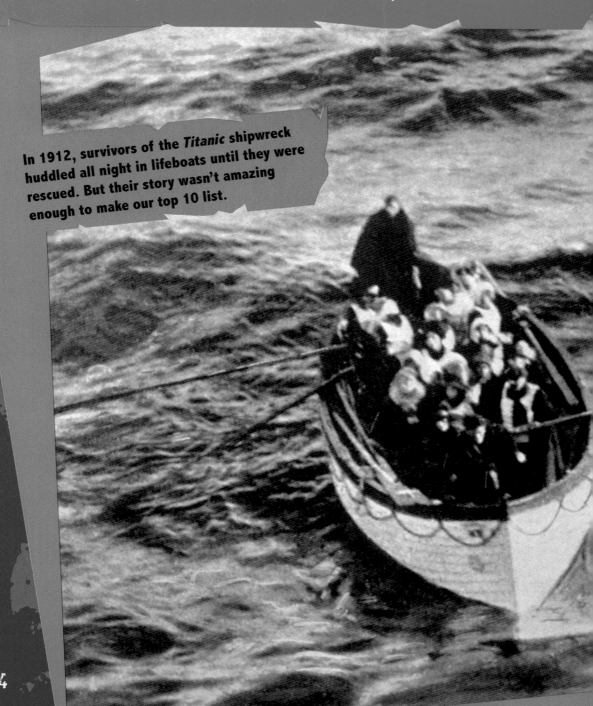

SURVIVAL STORIES

In 1912, survivors of the *Titanic* shipwreck huddled all night in lifeboats until they were rescued. But their story wasn't amazing enough to make our top 10 list.

People are born to survive.

When you crash on a bicycle, your hands try to break the fall. When you touch a hot stove, you quickly pull back. You don't have to think about these things. Your mind and body do them naturally.

The same is true for the people in this book. Faced with terrible circumstances, they did what comes naturally. They survived. But their tales are amazing because they were dealing with much more than a bicycle crash or a burned finger. Instead, they were dealing with life-or-death situations.

One lost an arm. Another cut off his arm. Some feasted on raw fish and bugs. Others ate human flesh. They did whatever was necessary to survive.

10 GARETH WOOD

Traveling across Antarctica is dangerous. But it was the jaws of an animal that nearly killed Gareth Wood. In November 1985, Wood joined Robert Swan and Roger Mear on an expedition to the South Pole. They arrived at the South Pole after 70 days.

Wood and his friends planned to sail back to New Zealand after reaching the South Pole. Their plans changed when the boat sank off the coast of Antarctica.

Wood reached the South Pole on
January 11, 1986.

The men planned to return to New Zealand by boat, but the boat sank before it could pick them up. Swan and Mear left by airplane. Wood stayed behind for another year with two companions to close down the base camp.

On April 17, 1986, the men went for a walk. As they crossed a frozen bay, they came to a crack in the ice. A large leopard seal burst from the crack and sank its teeth deep into Wood's right leg.

One of Wood's friends kicked the seal until it released its grip. As Wood tried to move, the seal again leaped from the water. More kicks sent it away for good. In December, Wood and his friends finally left Antarctica by airplane.

9

Nemcova still works to help tsunami survivors. Behind her are drawings done by children who survived the tsunami.

BORN: June 24, 1979

KNOWN FOR: Appearing in magazines such as *Sports Illustrated*, *Marie Claire*, and *Vogue*

FYI: In 2005, Nemcova told her story in a book called *Love Always, Petra*. She donated the sales from the book to tsunami victims.

PETRA NEMCOVA

In the blink of an eye, fashion model Petra Nemcova's dream vacation turned into a horrible nightmare.

On December 26, 2004, Nemcova and her boyfriend, Simon Atlee, were getting ready to leave the beach resort of Khao Lak in Thailand. The sky was blue and the sun was shining.

Suddenly, Nemcova heard screams. She ran to the window and saw people running from a huge wave. An earthquake in the ocean had caused a tsunami.

The wave crashed through the windows and swept Atlee and Nemcova away. Atlee disappeared under the wave. Nemcova managed to grab the top branches of a palm tree.

For the next eight hours, Nemcova clung to the tree. Bodies of people and animals floated past her. At sunset, rescuers reached Nemcova. Her pelvis was broken in four places, but she was alive. Atlee wasn't so lucky. His body was found about two months later.

8

O'Grady arrived at Aviano Air Force Base in Italy on June 9, 1995.

AGE IN 1995:   29

CALL SIGN: Basher Five-Two

WEIGHT LOST: 25 pounds (11 kilograms)

SCOTT O'GRADY

On June 2, 1995, U.S. Air Force Captain Scott O'Grady was flying a peacekeeping mission over Bosnia. But when O'Grady's F-16 fighter jet was blown apart by a surface-to-air missile, it was hardly peaceful. O'Grady escaped the flames and parachuted safely from 5 miles (8 kilometers) above earth. But he was deep in enemy territory. He knew that he faced torture or even death if enemy soldiers discovered him.

During the day, O'Grady hid in trees and bushes. He moved from place to place after sundown. Wearing only a thin flight suit, O'Grady was cold, hungry, and thirsty. He drank rainwater and plucked ants from a decaying worm for food.

Six days after his crash, O'Grady flipped on his radio and heard another Air Force pilot calling for him. They made contact at 2:06 in the morning. Four hours and 36 minutes later, a pair of Marine helicopters arrived to rescue O'Grady. At home, O'Grady received a hero's welcome.

7

Workers used a rescue capsule to lift the trapped miners to safety.

DATE OF ACCIDENT: July 24, 2002

MINE LOCATION: Somerset, Pennsylvania

FYI: Only one of the miners, Randy Fogle, still works underground.

QUECREEK MINERS

Dark, wet, and very cold. These were the conditions faced by nine Pennsylvania men in July 2002. As coal miners, they were used to working underground. But they weren't prepared to be stuck 240 feet (73 meters) below the surface for 77 hours.

That's what happened after the miners accidentally drilled through a wall into an old mine. The abandoned mine was filled with 50 million gallons (189 million liters) of water, which crashed through the walls into their mine.

The miners struggled through the passageways, trying to keep their heads above the cold water. They ended up in a small area at the highest point in the mine.

Meanwhile, rescue crews above ground worked to pump water out of the mine. At one point, the rescuers drilled a 6-inch (15-centimeter) pipe into the room where the trapped miners were staying. The miners tapped on the pipe to let rescuers know their location. Two days later, rescuers pulled the last miner out of the mine. All nine survived.

6

The shark that attacked Hamilton also took a huge bite out of her surfboard.

BORN: February 8, 1990

HOME: Kauai, Hawaii

STARTED SURFING: Age 5

FYI: Hamilton is homeschooled so she can concentrate on surfing.

BETHANY HAMILTON

The morning of October 31, 2003, started like normal for 13-year-old Bethany Hamilton. Her mother woke her up at 5:00 and asked, "Want to go surfing?"

Hamilton loved surfing, so the answer was an easy yes. Her mom dropped her off at the beach. Hamilton's friend Alana Blanchard was there with her father and brother.

As Hamilton waited for a big wave, she barely noticed a long, gray figure creep up beside her. Out of the water burst a 14-foot (4.2-meter) tiger shark. In one quick lunge, it bit off Hamilton's left arm.

The shore was a quarter mile (0.4 kilometer) away. Blanchard's father and brother helped Hamilton ride a wave to the shore. An ambulance took her to the hospital.

The shark attack became big news. People around the world were amazed that Hamilton survived. But they were even more astounded when she began surfing again only one month after the attack.

5

Doctors amputated both of LeMarque's legs just below the knees.

BORN: July 1, 1969, in Paris, France

CAREER: Played for the French Olympic hockey team in 1994

WEIGHT LOST: 35 pounds (16 kilograms)

FYI: Mammoth Mountain is part of California's Sierra Nevada mountain range.

ERIC LEMARQUE

Eric LeMarque loved the thrill that sports like hockey and snowboarding gave him. But on February 6, 2004, his desire for excitement almost cost him his life.

That afternoon, LeMarque went snowboarding alone. He plunged down the back of 11,000-foot (3,400-meter) Mammoth Mountain in California. When he stopped, he didn't know where he was. Night was coming fast. The temperature was dropping. LeMarque had no food and wore an unlined jacket. His cell phone battery was dead.

LeMarque spent the next several days searching for a path to safety. He used his snowboard to cut pine branches for bedding. He ate tree bark. But his feet were cold and wet, and he was running out of strength.

On February 11, LeMarque's family reported him missing. Two days later, rescuers found LeMarque huddled in a shelter he had built of snow.

Both of LeMarque's legs were amputated below the knees because of frostbite. Someday, he hopes to use his prosthetic legs to snowboard again.

4 STEVE CALLAHAN

Steve Callahan loved sailing alone. He found it peaceful. But Callahan found himself floating alone for far longer than he had ever imagined.

In 1982, Callahan was sailing in a boat he built. His goal was to sail all around the Atlantic Ocean. As Callahan sailed from the Canary Islands to Antigua, a storm tore apart his boat. He quickly boarded an inflatable life raft. He had food and water to last about 15 days. But his rescue would take much longer.

For more than two months, Callahan floated in the Atlantic. He ate raw fish that he caught with a fishing spear. He baited birds to his boat with pieces of fish and caught them with his bare hands. He had two solar stills that converted salt water into drinking water. When the stills wore out, he used a tarp to collect rainwater.

After 76 days at sea, Callahan drifted into the Guadeloupe Islands of the Caribbean. Fishermen saw birds in the sky and thought there must be fish in the water. But they didn't find fish. They found Callahan. He was thin, exhausted, and weak—but he was alive.

Callahan used a sextant made of pencils to help him navigate during his ordeal at sea.

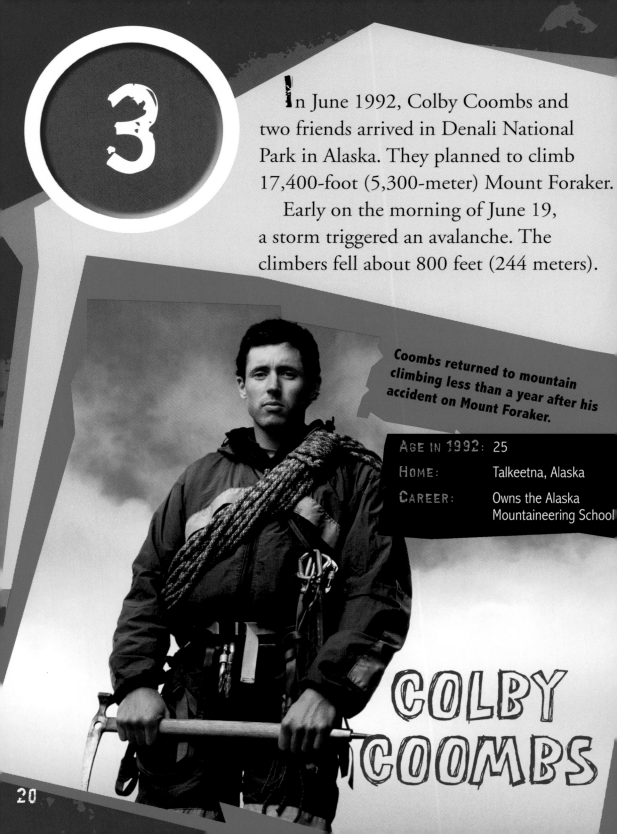

3

In June 1992, Colby Coombs and two friends arrived in Denali National Park in Alaska. They planned to climb 17,400-foot (5,300-meter) Mount Foraker. Early on the morning of June 19, a storm triggered an avalanche. The climbers fell about 800 feet (244 meters).

Coombs returned to mountain climbing less than a year after his accident on Mount Foraker.

AGE IN 1992: 25

HOME: Talkeetna, Alaska

CAREER: Owns the Alaska Mountaineering School

COLBY COOMBS

Coombs took this photo of himself as he made his way down the mountain after the avalanche.

Coombs was knocked unconscious. He woke up six hours later. Bones in his shoulder, ankle, and neck were broken. Worst of all, both of his friends were dead.

Coombs knew that his only chance to survive was to get off the mountain. For five days, he inched down the slope. He hurt too much to sleep, but he wanted to live. On June 24, Coombs reached the base camp. Doctors were amazed that his injuries didn't leave him paralyzed. As soon as he healed, Coombs returned to climbing mountains.

Survivors of the Andes plane crash huddled in the airplane's wreckage for warmth. This photo was taken after their rescue on December 21, 1972.

AIRPLANE: Fairchild F-227

PASSENGERS: 15 members of the Old Christians rugby club, plus family members and friends

FYI: The survivors gather every year on December 21.

URUGUAYAN RUGBY TEAM

On October 12, 1972, members of a rugby team boarded a plane in Montevideo, Uruguay. The players headed to a match in Santiago, Chile.

The plane crashed into the snowy Andes Mountains of Argentina. Ten people were killed instantly. The 35 remaining passengers were injured, cold, and hungry. Rescue teams searched for eight days, but they couldn't see the white plane in the snow.

The passengers had a small supply of wine, jam, and chocolate, but that soon ran out. Meanwhile, more passengers died. Eight were killed one night when an avalanche flooded the plane with snow. The remaining passengers survived by eating the flesh of those who had died.

After two months, two players went to find help. The men hiked 50 miles (80 kilometers) through the snowy mountains. On December 21, a farmer found them. Helicopters brought the 14 other survivors off the mountain to safety.

1

ARON RALSTON

BORN: October 28, 1975

CAREER: Worked for five years as a mechanical engineer

BOOK: *Between a Rock and a Hard Place*

Ralston took this photo of himself two days after becoming trapped in the canyon.

Aron Ralston instantly knew he was in trouble.

On April 26, 2003, the 27-year-old was canyon climbing in Utah. As he stood in a narrow slot canyon, an 800-pound (360-kilogram) boulder came loose, pinning his right hand against the rocky wall.

Ralston used all of his strength to push against the boulder. But he was stuck. His hand was badly crushed. The circulation of blood to his right arm was cut off. Ralston had little food and water. He began drinking his own urine. He used his video camera to tape a farewell message to his family and friends.

After six days, Ralston made a drastic decision. To survive, he would have to cut off his arm. He swung his body up and down, like a lever. One at a time, he broke each of the two bones in his forearm. Next, he wrapped his right arm in a tourniquet. He cut through the flesh with a dull pocketknife.

Free, but bleeding heavily, Ralston had to find help. He rappelled 66 feet (20 meters) to the canyon floor and walked 6 miles (9.7 kilometers) before finding a family of hikers.

Doctors fitted Ralston with a prosthetic arm. A few months after the accident, he was again doing the things he loved best—skiing, mountain biking, and climbing.

10

GARETH WOOD

9

PETRA NEMCOVA

SCOTT O'GRADY

8

7

QUECREEK MINERS

BETHANY HAMILTON

ERIC LEMARQUE

5

6

STEVE CALLAHAN

3

4

COLBY COOMBS

2

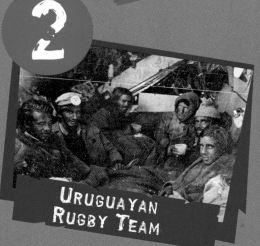

URUGUAYAN
RUGBY TEAM

ARON RALSTON

1

UNDERSTANDING SURVIVORS

The human brain and body know how to live. Some scientists call this the "survival instinct." Faced with deadly circumstances, the brain can choose to ignore pain and focus simply on staying alive.

That's why Bethany Hamilton was able to calmly swim to shore after a shark bit off her arm. It's also why Aron Ralston was able to slowly cut off his own arm. It explains how Colby Coombs hiked with broken bones, and how Steve Callahan floated for endless days under the hot sun.

People have the will to survive, but not everyone can perform feats this astounding. Survivors choose to do the best they can. They take action, and they fight to live. That's why the people in this book are truly the world's most amazing survivors.

Clear thinking can help people survive disastrous situations.

GLOSSARY

avalanche (AV-uh-lanch)—a large mass of ice, snow, or earth that suddenly moves down the side of a mountain

expedition (ek-spuh-DISH-uhn)—a long journey for a certain purpose, such as exploring

prosthetic (pross-THET-ik)—an artificial part that takes the place of a body part, such as an arm or leg

sextant (SEKS-tuhnt)—an instrument that uses the distance between the horizon and the moon, sun, or stars to determine a ship's location at sea

tarp (TARP)—a heavy waterproof covering

tourniquet (TUR-nuh-ket)—a tight wrapping designed to prevent a major loss of blood from a wound

tsunami (tsoo-NAH-mee)—a series of very large waves caused by an underwater earthquake or landslide

READ MORE

Hamilton, Bethany. *Soul Surfer.* New York: Pocket Books, 2004.

O'Grady, Scott, with Michael French. *Basher Five-Two.* New York: Doubleday, 1997.

Rohr, Ian. *Survival Against the Odds.* Real Deal. Philadelphia: Chelsea House, 2005.

INTERNET SITES

FactHound offers a safe, fun way to find Internet sites related to this book. All of the sites on FactHound have been researched by our staff.

Here's how:

1. Visit *www.facthound.com*

2. Choose your grade level.

3. Type in this book ID **0736864377** for age-appropriate sites. You may also browse subjects by clicking on letters, or by clicking on pictures and words.

4. Click on the **Fetch It** button.

FactHound will fetch the best sites for you!

Index